Experience Beyond Thinking

A Practical Guide to
Buddhist Meditation

Diana St Ruth

BUDDHIST PUBLISHING GROUP

Buddhist Publishing Group
Sharpham North, Ashprington,
Totnes, Devon TQ9 7UT, England.

ISBN 0-946672-26-1

A catalogue record for this book is available
from the British Library.

Printed and bound in Great Britain
by The Cromwell Press.

Dedicated to my brother

John

I would like to thank Don Whitbread, Dick, and the Sharpham Trust, all of whom have provided the expertise and the conditions necessary for the production of this book.

Contents

Introduction

I used to be bad at waking up in the mornings and would consistently be late for work. A neighbour who knew of my difficulty presented me with a repeater alarm clock for my twenty-first birthday. The alarm, I remember, was appropriately named 'Big Ben' and had a very large bell built into it which would raise the roof whenever it went off; then it would fall silent for a few seconds, and then off it would go again . . .

To begin with it worked wonders and I was getting up at the proper time every morning, for who could sleep through that? But, you know, I actually didn't want to leave my nice warm bed, especially on cold mornings, and so my subconscious mind invented reasons for ignoring it. I began sometimes not to hear the alarm at all, loud as it was, or to convert the urgent sounds into something innocuous. On one occasion the intermittent ringing became a fire engine racing down the road. And on another, the first burst of rings meant I was to wake up, while the second burst cancelled out the first and meant I could carry on sleeping!

My mind played elaborate tricks in order to escape the truth of what was happening and to remain unconscious. Eventually, the day came, however, when I had to make a firm decision within myself to wake up when my alarm went off and to get to work on time, otherwise I was going to lose my job. As soon as the decision was made deep within myself, I did it.

Meditating is a bit like that; it is similar to arousing ourselves from a very deep sleep. It can be difficult sometimes to wake. We keep sleeping, dreaming beautiful dreams, or even suffering torments in horrendous nightmares — anything but waking up. We know it is time, but we don't really want to do it. We read books, listen to talks, think about what other people say and yet don't actually do anything. We manage to convert all the information we gather into something ineffective, which then allows us to continue sleeping.

Do you want to wake up from the dream of life? Taking up meditation will be the deep decision within yourself which makes this possible.

Initially, meditation is a process of freeing the mind of its entanglements, of learning how to undo the knots. When I say 'mind' here I mean mind and heart both, because the two are but one. When the mind is opened and the heart is softened, something begins to function within oneself which liberates the self from the self —

one becomes liberated from oneself and, in consequence, liberated from the restricted world of the deluded mind.

Meditation is a way of being aware of everything experienced in life and also of recognizing the space in which life takes place; it is a process of becoming conscious of the obvious as well as the hidden, where all the mystery lies.

Awareness is the key. But what does the word mean to you? To most people, perhaps, it denotes an acknowledgement of that which is going on around them in a general sort of way. In the context of meditation, however, it means 'waking up', becoming acutely sensitive, knowing, feeling, living the moment in its pristine state, sensing colours and contours, sounds, textures, smells, recognizing tendencies within oneself yet resisting the pull to be controlled by them — this is meditation, to begin with at least.

Becoming aware of what happens deep within oneself may reveal the fact that there is very little real happiness there. Hoping, wishing, dreading, — there may be plenty of that, but genuine happiness . . . ?

Life is a bit of a game really, isn't it? We look forward to something and when it comes we criticize it, resent it, worry about it, want to change it, want to make it better.

For the most part, one's dreams are never fulfilled, and for the rest they are never quite right. I am talking now of the material world — the house, the car, the spouse, the children, the job, the status, the fun, the security, the health. It isn't a question of how much one has, but of how much real joy there is in it.

Why do so many beings have to endure hunger and cold, heat, disease, cruelty, physical and mental abuse and deprivation, torture, injustice, and all the rest of it? Some have to go through a living hell, don't they? And others suffer because there isn't any cheese in the fridge.

Why do I suffer? Is it the pain that makes me suffer? . . the lack of food? . . the lack of energy? . . . the lack of love? Is it oppression, dominance, the power of another that makes me suffer? Is it something out there? Or is it on the inside? Could it be that I suffer because of me?

The Buddha, a brave man, spoke the answer, but his words were expressions of something far beyond himself. He made the point clearly that whatever he said should not be taken as truth, but as an indicator, a signpost, a finger pointing to something beyond. 'Each person,' said the Buddha, 'must realize and experience truth for himself or herself,' otherwise what is it? Nothing but an idea — a useless concept floating around in a sea of confusion. So the Buddha expressed what he experienced. 'We suffer,' he said, 'from wanting what we do not already have.' 'Yes,' you may say, 'and what else?' Well, nothing else. That seems to be it. The cause of all suffering is yearning, wanting, wishing, desiring. It doesn't sound much of a reason. What about the husband? . . the wife? . . the job? . . the weather? What about the pain in my arm? What about the boy who committed suicide?

It sounds a bit glib to say they are what they are, but that is the truth of it. The boy committed suicide and any amount of wishing and wanting will not change that. The only thing I can control is my relationship to that fact. The decisions I have in life are related to how I live this moment, what I do and say now. I cannot change the past, arrange the future to suit myself, or make other people say and do the things I want them to say and do. All of my power is contained within this moment, related to this particular body and mind. And this is a very powerful position to be in.

There is no point in pondering a lot of 'truths' and discussing them with others on an intellectual level without ever trying them out for yourself. The tendency may be to hesitate and procrastinate, put it all off until tomorrow, talk and think about other people, how *they* should be, while never entering your own world.

'Enlightenment has waited this long, it can wait one more day. In the meantime, I want to finish wall-papering the back bedroom, go and see that film I've been waiting to see for months, and get in touch with Nick about the terrible job he did on my car.'

The time may come, however, when one more day is one day too long, when this life just isn't worth it any more, and when the inspiration rises up in one's heart to step out of the old routine and into something completely new.

What is presented here in this small volume is drawn from my own experiences of Buddhist meditation practised over a span of some twenty-odd years with numerous good and wise friends.

Anyone who wants to meditate can, but some have psychological needs which are not necessarily met by delving into the labyrinths of the mind unassisted. Do what is right for you.

I have enjoyed putting this book together. I hope you will enjoy reading it and of converting the word, which is but a symbol, into truth which is to be realized.

Diana St.Ruth
Sharpham
August 1992

What is Meditation?

Methods

There are many methods of Buddhist meditation being taught throughout the world today, but my belief is that the Buddha himself didn't teach any method at all. Here was a man, assuming there was such an individual (and all the evidence points to it), who is said to have walked out on his beloved wife and small son, and on an entire kingdom (he was an Indian prince), in order to take to the road in rags without a penny to his name.

The Buddha turned his back on material comforts, on his family, on the priests, and even on the holy men he met along the way whose wisdom, he felt, did not reach the mark. He refused to toe the line with anyone because his questioning was too deep, too real, too powerful. He sat alone, accompanied merely by his own deep honesty and awareness, and refused to move until the barriers to truth were shattered.

His method, according to the sutras (the dialogues and discourses of the Buddha), was to let the mind settle and the eyes of the inner being to open, to sit in stillness and be mindfully aware, allowing first one thing and then another to arise and pass away, clinging to no experience whatsoever.

Over the centuries all sorts of elaborate practices have been built onto this simple approach — mantras, koans, visualizations, prostrations, chants, bows and so on. It isn't that such forms, rituals and implements are not beautiful, helpful, true and valid (I have certainly found them to be so), but they are not always the direct way of proceeding for everyone. And for some, they may even prove to be a diversion which could engage them for the rest of their lives to little advantage.

The point is, anything can be used which is helpful to you. If the effects are negative and the practices begin to use *you,* however, then something is not right. Try not to be used by practices, teachings, or teachers!

Buddhism, I am sure, was never meant to be an 'ism'. One wonders what the man himself would have to say today if he saw what had grown up in his name, the man who chose freedom from ritual and dogma and the tainted views of others, the man who broke free of the constraints of family, teachers, followers, and the clinging defilements of his own mind. The Buddha laid great emphasis on encouraging others to look into themselves for themselves and to rely on that — something nonhuman, something unborn, unmade, something beyond culture and creed and the value judgements of oneself and others.

The Buddha didn't really have a method other than awareness, and awareness is no method at all; it is a straightforward 'opening of the eyes', a kind of waking up as if from a dream. That is all! But that is everything.

Experience Beyond Thinking

It is our habit to think about things, so much so that we practically ignore the things we are thinking about. I can look into your eyes and think about you, but not really see you. I can think about what it was like in the past for us and what it could be like in the future. The mind can drift on a sea of associated ideas, internalizing people and objects and looking at them from there.

When we live in the world with our minds full of thoughts, we don't sense much more than those thoughts; objects are not seen very clearly because the focus of our attention is directed towards what is in the mind rather than what is in front of our faces. Forms, at such times, are blurred and colours are dull. Tastes, sounds, smells, sensations — all distorted and indistinct when the mind is busy thinking. If we think about what we see, hear, smell, taste and touch, instead of just seeing, hearing, smelling, tasting and touching, we do not get the full flavour of the experience.

Try doing a job, any job, without thinking about the job itself or anything else besides. Simply stay with the body. Focus on a pair of shoes, for example, without saying 'shoes' in the head. Look at the shoes and know them for what they are, resisting the temptation to form a mental image of them in your mind, or saying the word silently to yourself. Put the shoes on without telling yourself what you are doing. Stay with the process, the action in the body. Avoid functioning from inside the head. Allow the action to do itself very naturally in the body. That is experience without thought, beyond thought; it is undistorted and unadulterated experience; nothing has been added to the process, and nothing taken away.

If I plunge my hands into steaming hot water, I don't need to think about whether the water is hot or not! I don't need to tell myself, 'Oh! I've scalded my hands.' Instantly — there is the answer as the pain rushes excruciatingly through my body. Knowledge does not come from thinking, as so many people do believe. It is with us all the while, naturally.

All situations are immediately known for what they are without the aid of thought. In fact, thinking usually only confounds the mind. So why do we do so much of it? Because we believe we have to, and because it is our habit to do so. With practice, however, we can learn to trust nature a little more. This is what we do in meditation.

Thinking is, of course, part of life too, and in certain forms it is invaluable. Wisely reflecting, skilfully planning, contemplating — these are creative forms of thought; but this is not the kind of thinking I am talking about, and it is not the sort most of us engage in for most of the time. The majority of us, it seems to me, tend to spend a good deal of our lives anxiously churning over what has happened, or what is about to happen. And some of us from time to time become attached to particular thought patterns and become obsessed by them, giving them enormous energy and power so that they sap our strength and overshadow everything we do.

There I am driving along Baker Street on a Monday morning in the thick of the traffic, but part of me is not there at all, part of me is thinking about a friend who is going off to India the following day, and I am wishing I could go too. I walk into the office, brush past the porter at the desk who is about to say hello, my mind still full of India. I talk on the phone, but am not really concentrating on what I am saying because my mind is besieged by a longing for India.

I have become obsessed by a thought and if I am not careful it will grow out of all proportion and spoil my life much more than it has done so up to this point. The drive, the porter at the desk, the office, the person at the other end of the telephone, are all vague and lifeless. This is how I can shun the world in favour of a shadowy realm of thought. Even if my world is a very bleak one it is a poor exchange.

Passing thoughts arise — that is natural, and they can bring us inspiration. But when one indulges in those passing thoughts, attaching to them, wallowing in them, getting caught up in them, they link up into a sort of chain of hopes, fears, doubts, anxieties, views and opinions. A strange view of 'self' arises from such a process and this kills the true self which bears no name.

Fears, worries, anxieties — all a result of thinking too much. Experience itself is separate from thinking about it; it is beyond thought.

'Drink a cup of tea,' as they say in Zen. Don't think about drinking a cup of tea — just drink it. Taste it. Feel it. Enjoy it. That is experience beyond thought. How nice! How free!

A Training?

Courses of training have certain values at times for people, but if Buddhist meditation is reduced to a training course for the purposes of strengthening one's powers of concentration and attaining spiritual goals, then the point of it will be completely missed. One can train oneself to sit, of course, in the full lotus posture without moving even a hair for hours on end, and that will, indeed, improve one's powers of concentration, but the inner eye will not be opened on that account.

Becoming very proficient, sitting beautifully just like a buddha, will impress our friends, perhaps! And if others are not impressed, we shall impress ourselves. We are stalwart 'practitioners', never missing a session. Ten, twenty years go by, but what have we achieved? A lovely posture! A serious countenance! An obsession! A lot of pride! And maybe a lot of hidden anxiety too because deep down we shall know something is amiss and that, in truth, nothing at all has been achieved. To acknowledge this deep fear would, in itself, be an insightful experience which would bring some form of liberation from the confines of the self and its ambitions, but we don't know this yet.

Freedom, wisdom, happiness — these are nobody's to possess; they are not the prizes of the spiritually muscle-bound, the serious young men and women with the straight backs, the quietly proud, and the holy. Ambitious pursuits (and taking up meditation as a form of training certainly falls into that category) block realization because they are forces aimed at imagined goals.

We need a structure in order to begin, yes, and we need a timetable and a degree of discipline, most likely, but let us not misuse the props. And let us not count up the sitting hours as credits towards a degree in complete enlightenment to be awarded in later years, or in the next life.

Unless one's motive for meditating is in order to wake up to reality in this moment, then it is doubtful if anything other than a sort of sleep, or negative mental state will come about as a result of it.

The Guru

The Buddha said, 'See for yourselves,' and it is my belief he said this as someone who was giving sound advice to his fellow human beings in a friendly and compassionate manner. His instructions were based on pointing to the true teacher within each individual, the true spiritual guide. When he meditated and became buddha himself, he wanted others to do the same — to be buddha themselves. That was his aim; no other.

There are some so-called spiritual advisors in the world today who try to persuade their followers to obey them without question, to act like servants, and to subject themselves to their 'wise' counsel in all matters. Needless to say, if people want to attach themselves to a spiritual guide and to idolize such a person, it is not the fault of the spiritual guide, but it is a little suspect if such a person actively encourages this.

I doubt that wise and compassionate human beings ever regard themselves as superior or in the slightest bit different from the meanest creature in existence. And I doubt that such beings would want anything less for others than the total release from the bondages of their own minds. It is, therefore, up to each one of us when coming into contact with gurus, however well established they are and wherever they are, to ascertain the genuineness of these people. Do we sense that a degree of wisdom and compassion is active in them? And do they seem to be *really* interested in the welfare of others, or is it only that they are interested in the welfare and promotion of themselves?

There are many fakes and many disillusioned individuals around who are thirsty for power and the adoration of others. Such people may have something to teach, but they may also have many psychological problems within themselves which they fail to recognize.

We have to assess whether a guru is a guru and we have to do it while remaining aware of our own possible resistances, conditioning and irrational hang-ups which could lead us either into disastrous associations, or into cutting ourselves off from sources of great wisdom. It could be quite a dilemma! Is he really a guru, or not? Is she really wise, or is it a show?

In order to find out we need to proceed with caution, but when all said and done, 'I' am the delusion which blocks out reality; 'I', this mythical 'me' is the cause of all our sorrow. We are standing in our own light; we are eclipsed. The real teacher is here in the centre of our being, pointing outward and inward simultaneously.

If we adopt teachers and teachings over and above this reality, we are simply avoiding the truth and exchanging our own set of useless views and opinions for someone else's.

Idolizing gurus, becoming attached to special people, handing over the responsibility of one's own life to someone else, relying on others to such an extent that one is unable to make a decision for oneself, is bondage, not freedom.

If one is meant to meet wise and compassionate people it will happen in a natural way without going in search of them. It isn't essential to have a personal guru or teacher; many do not. In actual fact everybody one meets, every thing, is a guru because life is teaching us something all the while. The universe ceaselessly offers up its reality in a multitude of forms. All one has to do is accept it as it comes. The guru is here all the while.

The Purpose of Meditation

I deas and concepts form pseudo-realities within the mind screening off the living truth and establishing us in ignorance. The nature of ignorance, of course, is such that we don't know we are ignorant, otherwise we would not be so! It needs something to reveal it to us, and this is where meditation comes in.

Meditation is the great antidote to ignorance. It allows us to see ourselves plainly as we are, as if standing before a large clear mirror. Nothing is hidden.

No matter how much we think, debate, or philosophize, we shall never find truth. If we begin with a concept, we shall end up with a concept. And concepts are not truths; they are brain patterns projected on the screen of imagination. This is not to say that truth is not translated into concepts, but the conceptual mind has to be dropped totally before truth is revealed just as it is.

Seeing into the mirror of the mind, therefore, is what meditation is all about.

*Meditation allows us to see ourselves clearly as we are, as if standing
before a large clear mirror.*

HOW TO MEDITATE

Awareness

If the movements of the body and mental processes are observed intelligently and with an open mind, one soon becomes aware of the mystery in life.

Clearly observing what is happening as it happens, not concerning oneself with what is not within one's field of consciousness, acknowledging the facts before one in a simple and direct way is the easiest, yet the most difficult, thing in the world to do — easy because one doesn't do anything except let nature take its course, and difficult because it isn't one's habit to allow that to happen; we like to interfere with our thoughts.

If only we could perform actions without getting involved in thoughts! By remaining alert to what is taking place from moment to moment, we discover a side to life which is both liberating and profound. Within that happy state of being lies the potentiality for unlimited compassion and wisdom. Neither the body, nor the natural thought processes, nor the world in any of its guises turns sour when we allow thoughts to flow like a stream — coming and going, coming and going — without hanging on to any of them.

When sitting, be fully in the sitting; feel the body sitting. Be aware of movements involved in walking. Be aware of standing. Be aware of lying down. Really get into the body; feel being the body; experience all its sensations — pressure, heat, cold, itching, tingling, aching, pain.

When taking a meal, for example, bring your attention to the smell of the food, to its appearance and texture. Attraction, indifference, repulsion — recognize these sensations as they come into existence. When eating utensils strike the plate, acknowledge their sounds. As food enters the mouth, feel it and taste it fully.

Let the body experience itself. This is the way to be liberated from the body. It's a paradox! To be with the body completely is to be free of it totally. The same is true of the world and the mind. Awareness brings this realization in daily life and in formal sitting meditation.

Practising awareness in another sense is practising recollection. We have to remember to pay attention. Washing, dressing, looking, speaking, feeling, sensing, listening, eating, tasting, touching — it is so easy to forget to live with even the pleasant and beautiful moments in our lives, let alone the unpleasant ones! The tendency is to slip into a separate world of thought, without ever noticing what we are doing. And then we miss the depth of the experience, whatever it may be.

Awareness is the practice of putting energy into staying with all experiences and impressions as they occur. And by doing this, gradually, one begins to notice how the mind works. It may come as a bit of a surprise to discover, for example, that intention is at the root of any action. There is the intention to walk before taking a step; there is the intention to speak, the intention to work, the intention to lose one's temper before it happens. When the mind decides, the body acts. The body responds, therefore, to visions in the mind.

Try slowing down a little when you move and then notice intentions as they arise; name them (silently to yourself) and then be aware of and name the actions which follow:

Intending to stand, standing; intending to walk, walking; intending to raise the arm, raising . . . and so on.

As we become accustomed to noticing intentions in the mind, we shall be giving ourselves the opportunity to change those intentions. We don't *have* to lose our tempers if we see the intention there before it has been acted upon; we can let it go, drop it so that it never comes to fruition. We may not want to drop it, of course, but that is our choice. At least we shall be giving ourselves the opportunity of making that choice and of realizing that we are not victims of our own tendencies and previous conditioning; we can change if we wish.

Attending to actions and naming them is merely being aware of normal everyday activities, but in a precise way. The naming should be silent, in the mind, and not spoken out loud.

In the same way, emotional states can be acknowledged for what they are — anxiety, confusion, happiness, sadness, hopefulness, fear . . . How are you now? Happy? Sad? Neither happy nor sad? Be aware of it; say it to yourself. Know the position of the body and know the state of the mind as much as possible throughout the day.

Jealousy, hatred, excitement, bliss, anger, grief, despair — when one of them comes, try to identify the feeling accurately and without attempting to do anything about it. Sensations and emotional states want to live — let them. Then they will want to die. Let them die too. Give them space and respect, but not energy. This is done by simply being aware; it isn't a complicated process. Try to be open to the new moment which is about to begin as much as you can.

Powerful thoughts and emotions have a tendency to want to stick; there is something rather attractive about them, even the painful ones. But to be aware also has something powerful to offer and to let thoughts and feelings go is no great loss; the unborn will then take birth freely within you.

There is the intention to walk before taking a step.

Summary

Awareness in everyday life

Be aware of:
   actions,
   intentions,
   emotional states,
   mental and physical reactions.

Make an effort to remember to be aware.

Let the body be aware of itself.

Let things go — passing thoughts, opinions and emotional states.

Sitting Meditation

F ind a quiet place where you can be totally free of
interruptions — a room, if possible, or a small
corner of the house. Make it very clear to husband,
wife, children or anyone else living in the house, 'This
is a time I am not to be disturbed. Questions, telephone
messages and miscellaneous bits of information can wait
until I've finished.' Be very clear and firm, otherwise
your meditation will be tense and anxious as you sit in
wait for the door to open and a voice calling your name.

If the rest of the family think you are crazy, fine.
Confirm their worst fears. Yes, you are crazy and you
are very happy about that. You are about to embark on
an exciting journey and do not wish to be cheated out of
it by others' opinions. And don't feel guilty about taking
the time for yourself. It's funny how others can become
rather jealous of the odd moment one wishes to spend
alone. You may well be accused of being selfish,
irresponsible in your consideration of others, and of
wanting to escape reality. Don't be put off!

So you are in your quiet room and the door is shut.
You don't have to be alone, of course, if someone wants

to meditate with you, or if you want to meditate in a group. Indeed, group meditation can be encouraging and supportive, and a good atmosphere can develop in a room where a few people are meditating together.

Now a sitting posture is to be adopted. There are several to choose from. Find the one which is most suitable for you. Experiment.

This is a time I
must not be disturbed.

The Lotus Posture

The traditional lotus posture is very difficult for adults to adopt without a great deal of practice and effort, but this is the ideal position because it is firm, balanced and relaxed. However, do not force yourself into it.

Sit on a firm padded cushion with your legs stretched out in front. (You may have to experiment with the height of the cushion.) Draw in one foot (say the right foot), bringing the heel as close to the crutch as possible. Rest the right knee to the ground. Take hold of the left foot and bring it up onto the right thigh so that the foot, sole upwards, is tucked into the groin. Then let the left knee rest down onto the ground. Now bring the right leg out from under the left and let the left knee drop to the ground. Draw the right foot up onto the left thigh, positioning it, as with the left, as close to the groin as

possible, and relax the knee to the ground.

Ideally, the position of the legs should be reversed from time to time (one foot and then the other being brought up first — maybe after twenty or thirty minutes of sitting, or simply alternating from one session to the next). This helps to maintain a balance in the body.

The Half Lotus

Then there is the half lotus, which is almost as good, but for most people probably just as difficult to adopt.

Sit on a cushion of suitable height. Stretch both legs out in front. Draw in one foot (say the right) and bring the heel as close to the body as possible. Rest the knee to the ground. Take the left foot and draw it up onto the right thigh. Let the knee come to rest on the ground.

Reverse the position at appropriate times, as in the case of the full lotus posture.

Simple Cross-legged Posture

A nd finally, as far as the cross-legged postures are concerned in this book at least, there is a simple variation which many people find possible without too much difficulty.

Sit on a cushion. Take hold of one foot and draw the heel close in to the crutch. Take the other foot and pull it as close as possible to the first so that the two feet are touching and the two heels are in line with the middle of the body. Both knees should be on the ground.

Swap the position at appropriate times so that the other foot is drawn close to the crutch first.

Kneeling

1 f sitting cross-legged is unsuitable for you, then you may find it better to kneel. This can be done with the aid of a cushion which you straddle: or with the aid of a specially designed stool with a sloping top.

Sitting on a Chair

But for many people, the best way of sitting is simply on a chair! Use an upright dining chair and sit away from the back so that you do not lean. Tuck the feet under the chair a little so that they are not directly beneath the knees (this will give greater support).

If the chair is too high, place a cushion under the feet. This will prevent the edge of the chair digging into the backs of the thighs.

Alternatives

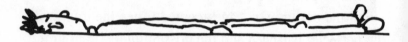

Lastly, if none of the above postures are attainable, then simply find one that is. It may be a matter of lying flat on your back. The important thing is to meditate, and in the final event any position will do.

A certain amount of experimentation may be needed in order to find the right position, one which can be held without too much difficulty for about twenty minutes. You may, of course, want to practise a posture at other times, one which you would like to be able to adopt, but cannot manage at the moment.

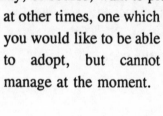

The Spine

1 f at all possible the spine should be erect, irrespective of the posture you have adopted. Then the trunk will be perfectly balanced and the possibility of strain in the back will be eliminated. Such a position can easily be maintained for many hours.

It may be worth getting someone else to correct your posture for you at some point, particularly the position of the trunk and back, because what to you feels straight, may not be!

The back of the head should be in line with the back of the neck; the head, therefore, tilts forward slightly.

The whole position needs to be balanced, firm, and relaxed.

Eyes

The eyes can be:

closed completely.

Almost closed, but not tightly, so that the eyelids are relaxed.

Open enough to look down at the floor a foot or so in front of you, without focusing on anything.

Hands

The hands can be held palms upwards, one on top of the other, loosely in the lap.

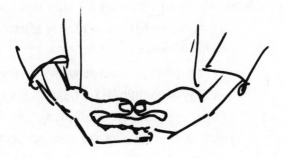

Duration

It is important to decide beforehand how long a session is to last, otherwise you will be thinking about it all the while and wondering, 'Shall I stop now?'

Ten minutes is probably enough initially and can be increased to fifteen or twenty after a few days or weeks.

At the end of some weeks of regular sitting, thirty minutes would probably be more appropriate. Following on from that, forty-five or sixty minutes may be a possibility. Practised meditators tend not to sit for more than this length of time in any one sitting. You must judge for yourself what feels right.

The duration of the sitting is no mark of progress; it is the quality of each moment which is important. If the sitting becomes an endurance test, therefore, it has lost its value and you will be wasting your time, or worse, you will be putting yourself off meditation altogether. Better to sit for a shorter period with enthusiasm and energy than to drag yourself through an hour faking it.

You will, of course, need some way of marking off the time. Traditionally, one might have sat for the time it takes to burn a stick of incense. You could do that if you like incense — many people do — but you would need to establish how long it takes to burn any particular kind of incense beforehand. Alternatively, you could use a nice 'quiet' alarm clock, or the alarm on your watch if you have one. Or, in the final event, simply glancing at a clock from time to time would be the thing to do, but this can be a bit of a distraction.

When to Sit

When is the best time of day to meditate? Some say first thing in the morning, others say last thing at night. You must find out for yourself. The deciding factor may not be the state of your mind, but a busy schedule, or the busy life of your family. The best time may, therefore, be in the middle of the afternoon when everyone is out, or at dawn when they are all still sleeping and the air is clear, or at ten o'clock at night when the kids are in bed and silence reigns.

You may like to sit more than once a day. Many people sit twice, or several times if they are on retreat. But one session of ten minutes is probably enough to be going along with. And give yourself a day off altogether once a week, otherwise you will feel trapped by it.

It is good to make a time for yourself to meditate, then you don't have to think about it any more. But try not to become obsessive about the time. I know of people who simply cannot get through the day unless they sit in formal meditation for the specified time, no matter what special circumstances arise. Their meditation takes precedence over everything, even matters which affect others seriously, and they will not be put off.

You can always postpone your meditation a little, or leave it until the following day; nothing will have been lost. It is quite obvious that if sitting meditation becomes time-oriented and nothing else, something has gone sadly wrong. Meditation is more than just sitting formally by oneself in a quiet room; it is noticing the condition of one's mind in any circumstances; it is becoming aware of the spontaneous uprising of life in each moment. Sitting in a special way is a form to be used for particular purposes, and a very powerful one if used correctly. But if one becomes obsessive about the time and the form alone with no regard to the content, then it is doubtful if it is working, i.e. that meditation is actually taking place at all.

There is no doubt, however, that unless one gives oneself the conditions for meditation and the space for it in one's life, then certainly it cannot work. And it is also a fact that the mind does not really want to face itself at any time and will invent reasons for not doing so. Try to be sensitive to what is going on, so that you do not enslave yourself to an ideal on the one hand, or mindlessly go through the motions by sticking rigidly to form, on the other.

Meditate when you can, when the time is right.

Concentration

You have appropriated a suitable place in which to meditate, and you have sorted out a nice posture in which to sit. The back is straight. The eyes are closed, or half closed. The hands are resting loosely one on top of the other, palms upward, in the lap. The physical side of things is all set. But what is happening in the mind? Is it calm and peaceful? Is it full of expectation? Is it chattering away to itself — imagining, wondering, worrying, planning?

An attempt should now be made to concentrate.

Counting breaths

Breathe in and count silently to yourself 'one'. Breathe out and count 'one' again. You have now counted one complete breath. On the following inhalation count 'two', and 'two' on the exhalation. Continue counting for ten full breaths. Then start again at 'one'. There may be some difficulty in retaining full concentration for the time it takes to breathe ten full breaths. The mind will probably wander. If it doesn't, I would be very surprised!

If and when the mind wanders, therefore, and the count is lost, simply begin again at 'one'. Should the counting become mechanical, again, go back to 'one'.

Another possibility is that you find yourself counting mindlessly beyond ten, and this will be a further indication of loss of concentration. Go back to the beginning again and again. You may find you can hardly reach 'two' before your concentration goes. It doesn't matter. Reaching 'ten' is not the object of the exercise. *Trying* to do it is the purpose. And in that effort much will be revealed and realized.

You may be surprised at your inability to control the mind for even a very short time. You may be amazed to discover just how much 'chatter' goes on in there, how many images form, how much flitting from subject to subject there is, or dwelling on one issue which invades the mind over and over again. You may find that you are unable to simply sit quietly and count a few breaths. The 'noise' and 'pictures' just won't stop!

Please don't become frustrated or depressed on account of this inability to control the mind. You are seeing how the mind works. You are discovering how *you* work. That is why you are meditating. Be interested in what you are doing and what you discover about yourself. Try to concentrate, but be aware of what happens in that attempt. Forgive yourself if you find your concentration is poor, and continue to make the effort. Make the effort, but without force; try to do it in a gentle way; gently bring the mind back to the exercise time and time again. Be patient with yourself. Let yourself be what you are, and try to stay with the counting. Be interested in doing this very simple thing in the moment. Be interested in counting breaths, and then all the other mental activity will abate. The mind will stay with what it is interested in. While the mind counts, it will not do anything else. This is one-pointed concentration. Be content to count for its own sake. So difficult! So easy!

As the counting takes place to the rhythm of the breath, the mind will be calm and clear, if only for a little while. That moment or two of clarity will be enough to reveal the value of concentration. Worrying, hoping, dreaming and wishing cannot occupy a space already filled with the counting of breaths. This is a simple revelation which has a deep significance, to be contemplated and fully realized. Just by concentrating in this uncomplicated way, one can come away from, or dissolve, a negative mind state, even if it is only for a moment.

Meditation is a way of facing deep and real issues and of experiencing their transformation into something positive and creative.

After a while, a degree of concentration and calmness will begin to manifest itself and develop. It is impossible to say how long this will take. For some it may be almost immediate; for others it may take weeks or months, or creep upon them imperceptibly over a longer period of time.

Then, when the time is right, the exercise can be dispensed with. But you must be honest with yourself.

Is it time to leave this exercise? Has it served its purpose? There is no point in waiting for perfection! You may *never* count ten breaths without faltering. It is enough to establish just *some* concentration, and to experience just *some* degree of clarity and calmness. If you wait for perfection — an uninterrupted flow of ten counts over and over again for twenty minutes or so — you may wait for a very long time! Move on when you genuinely feel it is time. Experiment if you like; you can always return to this exercise again in the future if you feel you need to. It is all a question of finding that balance between moving too fast and not moving at all.

Subjects of Concentration

C ounting breaths is practised by making words with the mind to mark off a physical action. The breath is observed and a word is formed about it. This is concentrating with the aid of thought.

These next exercises are also related to the breathing process, but from a slightly different perspective. Becoming aware of the sensations of breathing will draw the mind into the body and away from thoughts, though initially naming (forming thoughts about what is happening) may be useful to help concentration.

There are many variations on concentrating on the breathing process, but I will list just three. Only one of them is to be used — it doesn't matter which. They are all of equal value so there is no question of progressing from one to the other. Yet you may wish to try them all out as time goes by in order to see which fits the best. Finally, however, decide on one and stick to that.

1. Concentrating on the length of breaths taken. Is it a long, deep breath? Is it a short breath? Or is it neither long nor short?

2. Concentrating on the warm and cool sensations in the nostrils as the air flows through while breathing in (cool) and breathing out (warm).

3. Concentrating on the rise and fall of the abdomen (approximately three finger-widths below the navel) while breathing in (rising) and breathing out (falling).

The breathing is a continuous process while one is alive and for that reason a very convenient subject on which to meditate. An important point to remember, however, is that observing the breath is not an exercise in breathing, it is an exercise in observation. Please do not exaggerate or alter the breathing pattern. Simply breathe naturally and become conscious of that.

Alternative Subjects of Concentration

Sometimes people have difficulty with concentrating on the breath because as soon as they do so, it becomes strained and awkward. Basically, the breathing pattern relates to the state of the mind. When the mind is anxious, the breath will be tense and irregular too. When the mind is calm, the breath will flow evenly and gently, and may almost become imperceptible.

The breathing, therefore, reflects the condition of the mind at any point in time. That is another reason for using the breath as a subject of meditation — one sees how the mind affects the body.

If, after much perseverance, one really cannot get along with watching the breath as a subject, then choose something else. Sound is a good alternative. Even in the quietest places, sounds will be heard — birds, the wind, a train, a plane, the central heating system, and so on. But if meditating on sound begins to include getting involved in a conversation taking place outside the window, or the programme on next door's television set, then it is no longer of value.

It is better, of course, not to have to listen to someone else's sound equipment when meditating, so try to avoid it altogether, but if it should happen to invade your quiet space suddenly, then don't reject it either, at least for the duration of that session. Observe the sound as sound without getting drawn into the content of it, and without judging it as pleasant or unpleasant, or right or wrong. This, too, can be a very valuable exercise.

Other alternatives to watching the breath are meditating on a flowing stream, or the flame of a candle. But there aren't many people who can sit by a flowing stream very often, and staring at the flame of a candle can damage the eyes. So these things are not ideal on a long term basis.

Static objects — an ornament, a flower, the floor, the wall and so forth — are not good subjects either. It is all too easy to *think* while staring at something static, and not realize what is happening. This is why moving objects are

better. Movement needs constant attention for it to be followed.

Watch and Note
Without Judging

Now you have chosen a new subject on which to concentrate. Sit in the formal posture, relax into it as much as you can without slumping down, and just breathe. Feel the body sitting and breathing. Nothing else matters.

Now take up the exercise you have chosen from the three listed previously. Supposing you have decided that the rise and fall of the abdomen will be your main object, go to that area now and name the actions that are taking place. The physical movements may be very gentle and subtle, almost imperceptible. It doesn't matter. Don't increase them in an attempt to make them easier to follow. Simply become aware of the little movements there are. Feel the rise and fall, and say the words silently to yourself, 'Rising, falling, rising, falling,' as the abdomen moves. Make sure the words coincide with the actions and let the breath flow naturally.

inhalation/exhalation. There will be rest periods in between. Be equally aware of the gaps and the whole body in contact with the floor and the cushion, or the chair, at these times, and say 'sitting' to denote the experience. 'Rising, falling, sitting, rising, falling, sitting . . .'

Watch and note without judging. 'Good', 'bad', 'right', 'wrong' — these evaluations do not apply to the purity of what is taking place now, about which nothing need be said. When the attention wanders, note it and form the word in the mind — 'thinking'. Be fully aware that you have been thinking and that it has drawn you away from concentrating on the rise and fall of the abdomen. Take time to fully appreciate what has happened: 'Thinking, thinking, thinking.' Then go back to the main subject of meditation again: 'Rising, falling . . .'

Do not reject thought, sound, sensation, passion, or anything which arises in meditation. Accept it all. Acknowledge it, name it, feel it, and then redirect the attention back to the rise and fall of the abdomen (or whatever the main object of the concentration is). A period of sitting meditation may go something like this:

Rising (of the abdomen), falling, sitting, rising, falling, sitting, rising, falling, aching (of, say, the knee or ankle), aching, aching, aching, (and then return to the main subject again,) rising, falling, (the mind wanders), dreaming, dreaming, dreaming, rising, falling, sitting, rising, itching, itching, itching, rising, falling, wanting to swallow, intending to swallow, swallowing, rising, falling, sitting, thinking, thinking, thinking, rising, falling, pain, pain, pain, wanting to move, rising, falling . . .

Make the meditation subject the centre of your gravity, as it were. Zone in on it as much as you can. And whenever you find yourself dreaming about what you are going to have for tea, or about meeting an old friend in town, stop! Come back to yourself, to where you are and what you are doing. Acknowledge the truth of the moment and say to yourself, 'Dreaming, dreaming, dreaming' (or, 'planning,' or 'wanting,' or whatever it is that has been occupying you for the last few moments), and go home again to the subject of concentration. Do this whenever the occasion arises.

Try to maintain your sitting posture without moving. The idea is that the living moment can display itself, fulfil itself, only against an intelligent and sensitive stillness, without interference or interruption. For this, not only discursive thinking, but the body also should be inactive. Occasionally, however, particularly in the early days of meditation, an irritation or an ache can become intolerable. Make the decision to relieve the discomfort by moving or scratching the area in question. Then, slowly and mindfully do something about it, acknowledging each and every action as it takes place. 'Moving, moving, moving', as the hand, say, moves to the itch, 'scratching, scratching, scratching,' as the hand slowly scratches the itch, and then, 'moving, moving, moving', as the hand returns just as slowly to its original place. Finally, when the whole operation is completed, 'Rising, falling, sitting, rising . . .'

Keep up the naming process until the mind wanders less and less, and then leave the naming alone; it will have served its purpose. Move on!

The End of the Name

A ll aids to meditation must be dropped at the appropriate time, otherwise they will become too familiar, too comfortable and no longer of any value. An aid, in fact, can become a hindrance and lead to frustration and negativity if held on to for too long. Be ready to drop the naming when the time is ripe. Let the mind live in spontaneity.

Naming, which in the beginning is a powerful way of reminding the mind not to produce thoughts beyond what is happening, is still a thought-producing activity and as such sustains the false notion of a self — 'me' watching and naming 'it', the body. The rise and fall of the abdomen and the knowing of the rise and fall is not attributable to a self. The sound and the observer of it, the itch and the experiencer of it, do not involve a 'me' doing it. It is time to see that now.

When the naming stops, when the mind is quiet, all notions of a self also dissolve. The name, the thought, the label which is believed in, gives the illusion of a separate being — me and you. Once the name is seen as arbitrary, then it will simply be recognized as a name and nothing more.

Observe the rise and fall of the abdomen without thinking about it. Be totally at one with it. As the body moves, be the movement. Do not say to yourself, 'This is me sitting here now being aware of my breathing.' Do not observe the rise and fall and produce the words 'rise' and 'fall'. Become one with the breathing. Recognize all that comes, see it for what it is, but do that without slapping a label on it and making a story out of it. Feel the lightness rushing through the mind and body. Feel the freedom.

Feel the lightness.

Nonattachment

B e aware of the breathing (the rise and fall) and be aware of whatever else passes by — a sense, a feeling, a thought, a smell, a sound. Let the mind open. Observe, but not as someone watching. Try not to become involved in thoughts. Let them fulfil their function and then let them pass on, otherwise you will not be free.

There are no intrusions or disturbances for one who is really meditating. If you are drawn away from the main point of concentration by a sound, or an ache, or a moment of despair, or a simple thought, and feel that such is an intrusion into your special world of meditation, then frustration or anger will surely arise as a result. Be aware of that attitude and any accompanying frustration. Acknowledge the experiences as they arise. They are the reality of the moment.

There is no need to be disappointed or annoyed about being drawn away from the main subject of meditation. No crime has been committed. Welcome whatever comes! Then everything will be the meditation itself and will be regarded as an opportunity for change. This is turning the negative into the positive.

The mind, life itself, is crushed by clinging and rejecting. Clinging and rejecting — these are two sides of the same coin. They are the forceful, even violent, activities of the ego-centred aspect of this phenomenon

I Want you!   *Go away!*

I call 'me'. Have the courage to let a thought slip by and not chase after it. Not clinging to thought, not rejecting it, the mind will open to a natural awareness. And awareness moves where life moves, not where hopes, fears, and wishes move. Come away from the wandering dreamy mind into the reality of the moment and cling to nothing. Be totally free. This is a distinct possibility for you, for me, and for anyone who has the courage to trust life, forego the past, and allow the moment to be itself.

Pain

When one willingly accepts whatever feelings, sensations, smells, tastes, irritations, thoughts, or images that crowd into one's meditation, then no conflict will take place. That goes for physical pain too.

We reject certain sensations; we dislike them; we don't want them. Hatred, annoyance, impatience, anxiety, or resentment arise as a result of rejecting sensations. In an attempt to keep suffering at bay, therefore, greater suffering is experienced. If pain springs up while meditating, maybe in the knee or ankle, try to give it space in your consciousness without fear or ill will. Attend to the pain very carefully and observe it impersonally as though it belonged to someone else; simply let it be.

After a moment or two the pain may subside (pain usually comes in waves), in which case go back to the rise and fall. On the other hand, the pain may increase. If it does and becomes intolerable, then there is no point in struggling under the weight of it. Mindfully reposition the body and continue concentrating on the breath.

Bearable pain, however, can be a very useful subject on which to meditate. An ache, a pain, an itch, has life. Relax and let it live! It will not survive forever; nothing does. And here is an opportunity to look at pain, something you may normally regard as unpleasant, without regarding it as anything at all. Then you will experience pain without suffering.

Pleasure may be treated in the same way because pleasure is the inverse of pain. To yearn for pleasure

and to fear pain are the opposite poles of the same unsatisfactoriness.

Joy and bliss may also spring up and pervade one's being in meditation. This is a result of meditating on the body and not attaching to anything. Continue to be aware. Let the sensations come and go without interference. If you identify with bliss and indulge in it, grasping will enter into the situation and there will be a sense of loss and disappointment when the sensation departs, with an added feeling or desire for recreating it. If one works at recreating bliss, meditation will then have taken on a very dubious persona.

Bliss attained by willed effort will be cultivated, not spontaneous. And if you steal sweets that aren't being offered to you, they can make you very sick.

Nonattachment to all sensations — pleasant or unpleasant — is the route to happiness.

Summary

Sitting Meditation

Find a quiet place.

Set a time for the duration of the sitting.

Adopt a suitable sitting posture:
    cross-legged;
    kneeling with a cushion or stool;
    on a chair.

Eyes half or fully closed.

Rest hands loosely in the lap (palms upward, one on top of the other).

Counting Breaths

Inhale — 'one'; exhale — 'one';
inhale — 'two'; exhale — 'two' . . .
and so on up to 'ten'. If concentration is lost, begin again at 'one'.

. Continued

Subjects of Concentration

Choose one of the following.

(1) Concentration on the length of each breath — long, short, or neither long nor short.

(2) Concentration on the warm and cool air flowing through the nostrils (inhalation — cool; exhalation — warm).

(3) Concentration on the rise and fall of the abdomen (a point approximately three finger-widths below the navel).

Take up one of the above subjects. Acknowledge thoughts, feelings and sensations as and when they arise. Return to the main subject whenever possible.

Walking Meditation

Walking is a wonderful way of meditating. It brings one to the point of realizing that meditation does not depend upon the position of the body. Sitting, standing, lying down, walking — what is the difference when one is aware? The state of being aware is an experience which goes beyond the body.

The formal practice of walking meditation is very useful in retreat situations where a lot of sitting is taking place and the body is getting stiff. To walk for ten minutes or so, between periods of sitting, stretches the joints and can bring relief to aching knees, ankles and so on. But more than that, in a sense, walking meditation is like putting sitting meditation into motion. This can break down any misconceptions about meditation being something only to take place in perfect stillness.

Freedom from form, feeling, mental activity, perception and consciousness — this little bundle called 'me' — can be experienced at any time just by engaging in the business at hand in a meditative way, whether it be the rise and fall of the abdomen, or the placing of one foot in front of the other in walking meditation.

Stand upright and perfectly still.

Allow your arms to hang loosely by your sides.

Look at the ground far enough ahead to see where you are going, but don't study what you see.

Concentrate on the body, the whole body, standing.

Notice the intention to raise one foot.

Place your attention on that foot.

Raise the foot a little and momentarily hold it there.

Notice the intention to move the foot forward.

Move it forward and hold it for a moment just above the ground.

Notice the intention to place the foot to the ground.

Place it to the ground.

Now repeat the process with the other foot.

Persuade the mind to stay with the movements by reminding it what is going on. Say what is happening to yourself in the way that you do, initially, in the sitting practice: 'Intending to raise, raising, intending to move, moving, intending to place, placing . . .'

Continue walking for, say, fifteen steps, or until there is no more floor space. If the exercise takes place outside, find a suitable spot and limit the distance, otherwise you could find yourself enjoying a lovely walk somewhere, but not practising what you had set out to do.

At the end of the stretch of floor or path, stand for a moment or two. Be aware of the whole body standing. Produce the intention to turn. Notice that intention. And then turn slowly until you are facing the opposite direction. Now continue, walking back again.

Practise walking up and down slowly for ten or twenty minutes.

In sitting meditation one point only is focused upon with the acknowledgement of whatever else happens to arise. In walking meditation, however, many movements are observed. Each is taken slowly and deliberately and concentrated upon. Whenever concentration is lost, stand for a moment, re-establish the concentration, and then continue. There is no need to stop on account of every fleeting thought that passes the clear space of your mind, however. Spontaneous thoughts, sounds, smells, the wind in your face, the pressure under your feet will appear and disappear in your consciousness. Let them come and go as they please. Only if you become completely absorbed into some mind state, do you need to stop, allow the concentration to return to the body, and continue again at that point.

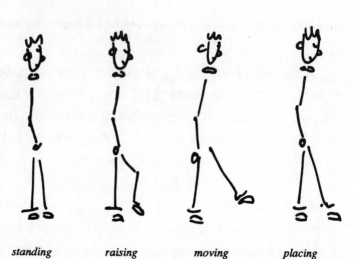

| *standing* | *raising* | *moving* | *placing* |

'Standing, standing, standing intending to raise (the foot), raising, intending to move (the foot), moving, intending to place (the foot to the ground), placing, intending to raise, raising, intending to move, moving . . .'

| *raising* | *moving* | *placing* |

Just before turning to walk back again, stand for a moment: 'Standing, standing, standing, intending to turn, turning, turning, turning, standing, standing, standing, intending to raise, raising . . .'

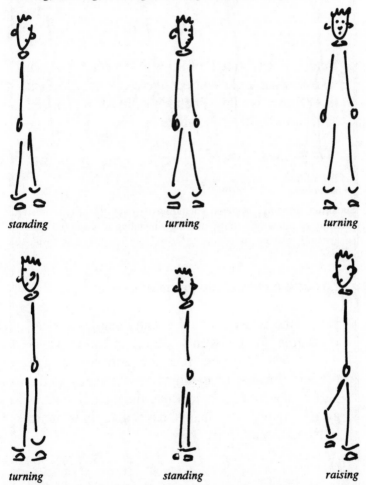

standing   *turning*   *turning*

turning   *standing*   *raising*

As with the other practices, naming the movements should be dropped in due course, so that you become aware solely of walking.

Summary

Walking meditation

Find a decent stretch of floor upon which you can take at least eight consecutive steps in a straight line (fifteen would be better), or locate a secluded spot in the open somewhere.

Set a time for the exercise (ten or twenty minutes).

The arms are to hang loosely by one's sides.

Stand perfectly still.

Lower the eyes to the ground just ahead.

Name the actions initially and then, when the inclination to stay with whatever is happening in the moment is greater than the tendency to drift off into dreams, imaginings, and thoughts of the past or the future, discontinue the naming and be aware simply of what is happening in a more immediate and direct way.

Just Sit

There will come a time in meditation when any subject of concentration, the rise and fall of the abdomen, or whatever it may be, will become more of a hindrance than a help in staying with the reality of the moment. How long will this take? That is impossible to say. It will be when the mind doesn't need anything to persuade it to stay open and awake any more; it will be when any use of persuasion, which in essence is what concentration is, will feel heavy and wrong. At such a time, there will be no desire to run into the past or the future, or anywhere beyond what is here and now.

When there is total acceptance of this moment, one hundred per cent, that is when all predetermined objects of concentration can and should be dispensed with, because that is when the eyes of the mind will be wide open.

Let go of all subjects of concentration and just sit. Thoughts will come and go, of course, and feelings and sensations, but behind those natural uprisings, a deep clarity of mind, an intense calmness and great energy will extend throughout one's being and throughout the whole field of consciousness. Sitting in meditation, being open to what comes, without thought-commentary, without feeling the need to tell yourself, 'That's the wind blowing in the trees;' 'That's a train passing;' 'That's the smell of toast;' 'That's a pain in my right knee;' 'That's a bird singing;' you just know these things before the voice of the mind speaks, before images are made. You know perfectly well what is taking place without telling yourself.

The echo of, 'Oh, what a beautiful sunset,' in our minds, removes us from the beauty. The, 'Oh, how dreadful it is that they suffer so much,' removes us from a deep inner connection with those beings. The essence of what we are knows what is going on without having

Thinking about the sunset.

it explained or repeated in code. In fact, only the essence of mind knows; nothing else does.

The body breathes; life is the way it is; no complications, no self, no other, no time, no birth, no death, no eternity, no annihilation, no one to breathe, no one to worry. Here — just sitting.

In awareness one sees and knows with a mind free of emotions, greed, hatred and delusion. It isn't that one loses the power to think, of course, and plan, and remember past events. It's just that one is moved by what one experiences rather than by what one thinks about.

There is a famous saying by a Zen master, 'When hungry, eat. When thirsty, drink. When tired, sleep.' To live in a simple, direct way, without cluttering up the mind with wanting things, hating things, judging, taking too much, avoiding one's duty, cutting off from reality and allowing the mind to become obsessed, dull, lost in a dream, worried, or full of doubt, is a wonderful experience, genuine happiness. And it's ours for the taking.

It is important to be sensible when formulating a programme for yourself from the exercises in this book; they are suggestions only, hints. You must find your own way, otherwise it will be like wearing someone else's coat which doesn't fit properly. Meditate freely.

LIVING TRUTH

Old Habits

When life becomes difficult, we can refuse to play the misery game; we can resist the pull to react to the vicissitudes of this human existence; we can keep from falling prey to black states. It is possible to be free of old habits by consciously deciding not to be dragged along by them.

Ask yourself: Am I tired of going through all this again — this mood, this misery I heap upon myself and others besides caused by repeating old life patterns, cycles of events which take weeks, months, years, maybe even lifetimes, to play themselves through? Have I had enough? Is my heart sick and tired? And am I not bored with going through the same old thing again and again and again *ad nauseam*?

What is your tendency? What gives you the most trouble? Find out. And does it ever occur to you that it is *you* who are bringing suffering upon yourself, not the outside world? Aren't you attracting destructive forces to yourself by the way you are? Can you break the mould?

Ask these questions of yourself. Contemplate your life so far and see whether it forms a pattern. Is it time to go on . . . learn the lessons and move in another direction . . . turn corners?

Through watching actions and reactions in meditation and in daily life, it will be possible to see into the conditioning which ruins your life. It is conditioning (habits formed by past experiences) which drive you into miserable states, impelling you to destroy what is beautiful and good. It is old habits which cause you to throw a wet blanket over that deep happiness which is available at this precise moment and is yours by right.

Is it you who are bringing suffering upon yourself?

'Me' and 'you' — these are terms used for ease of speech. But look into the fundamental notion of 'self' within your own being; examine the premise from which your life is lived. See the 'self' that stretches out its greedy hand to take from others and then to ask for more and more and more. 'Self' is greediness, hatred, foolishness personified; it is a word for ignorance and painful delusion; it is a belief which has no foundation.

When you can be at one with the moment without concentrating on anything in particular, the mind will not go blank and life will not suddenly disappear into a deep black hole, but neither will 'a person' be found dwelling inside the body with a name and position in life. 'The person' is seen to be a myth — not metaphorically, but actually — a fabrication of the deluded mind. There is life, yes, here it is; it is being experienced right now. But the person — who is that?

The Person: Me

What is it like in there? Is it dark? Is it cold? Is it full of bones, flesh and blood? Is it empty? Is it you? Who is it that owns that body? Does anyone own it? Who are you? Who am I? Who is sad? Who is happy?

Look intently at whatever arises — a sound, a sensation, a vision, a word, a smell. Observe. Be a silent witness to the moment. Watch the universe unfolding and be aware, totally open, awake. Put effort into bringing to consciousness what is sensed. You will see the mind and all that is contained within it. You will see that everything is contained in the mind including physical form. You will see that mind and body are transient, re-being in the present. You will see that mind and body are formed and unformed both at the same time.

For so long we have confused ideas with truth. But truth has no name, no description, no idea of itself. Thinking that 'I' exist in the body is to believe there is a separate being that is born and will die, an individual person who owns a body and mind. But what is the truth of that? What is really being experienced? Thoughts are experienced — images, sounds, sensations, smells, tastes — in the mind. They come into existence and they pass away. Feelings are experienced — sensations, emotional states, ideas — all are born and all will die. In meditation we see them coming into being and passing away, first one and then the other.

If anything permanent were to be found inside or outside of the body or mental processes, then it would be possible to say that the self had been found, but it isn't. The mind constructs the idea of a self, an entity living in the world separate from other entities, and this mental formation can and does wreck our lives. We act on it as a premise; we spend our time trying to make this self happy.

When awareness dissolves the tendency for concepts to arise, the 'I' state of mind dissolves like the early morning dew and the 'I' thought no longer takes a hold. 'I like . . . ;' 'I don't like . . . ;' 'I believe . . . ;' 'I don't believe . . . ;' 'I want . . . ' — in moments of awareness, the habit of producing a person to enjoy life or to suffer it is interrupted.

In ignorance we believe things. We believe we have selves in bodies — 'me'. It doesn't occur to most people that 'self' is a concept, just an idea, and that the notion of birth, ageing and death of 'self' are further developments of that original idea. Many beliefs, and the belief of 'self' is one of them, are fixed in our minds and affect us dramatically throughout our entire lives. We have trapped ourselves in a web of delusion.

Investigating the nature of existence by meditating is facing the *fact* of what is actually taking place as opposed to what one *believes* is taking place. That is all meditation is — a way of looking. It isn't a method of changing anything, or obliterating anything. Do you want to know? Then look! What are you afraid of?

The mind constructs the idea of a self.

There is life; it won't be removed just because it is being examined without prejudice. The meditator isn't going to face annihilation by seeing into what he or she is!

When the eye of the mind and heart is open, you will see that nothing that comes into being remains unchanged. Everything is impermanent; there is a constant coming into being and ceasing to be, and a self cannot be found in any of it.

The body, the mind — an empty space full of being.

The Unborn

In meditation all things are seen to be impermanent — they come and they go. And whatever comes and goes cannot be regarded as 'me', a self. But who is it that knows this? Who knows the birth and death of a sound . . . a sensation . . . a dream? Sound itself doesn't know sound. Sensation doesn't know itself. Something else does that. What is it? Is it thought, or the thinking mind? Does thought know? But I have already discovered through meditation, through the aware condition of my mind that thoughts are nothing but mental creations — memories, hopes, dreams, fears; they are forms which have been produced and are also known by something other than themselves.

A sound, a thought, a sensation, a dream — these are all born into existence and they all die. They are all born, but that which experiences whatever has been born — is that born? How can it be? Whatever knows the born cannot be born; it must be something else; it must be something unborn. Unborn, unformed, unmade, unproduced — it is that which is *not* which knows what *is*. And what is that? What is that which is not? This is the same as asking, 'Who am I?' And that is a good question too.

The experiencer, the perceiver, the knower of life, is close, personal, familiar; so much so that I believe it is myself. The unborn in which the born takes place — that and what I commonly regard as 'me to myself' — seem to be one and the same. Are they? Am I unborn? If I am, I cannot say it is me, can I? I cannot say that something unformed, unmade, without colour, texture, or shape, is a person — me! If I am the unborn, then so are you. I cannot say the unborn is me, but neither can I say it is not me.

A blind man can see. He can see darkness with the mind, not the thinking mind, but with the unborn mind. The blind man doesn't possess sight, but he possesses the perception of sight. The perception of sight is what one really sees with. The same is true of the perception of hearing, tasting, smelling, touching and thinking. The eighth-century Zen Master Hui Hai was questioned:

> *When there are sounds, hearing occurs. When there are no sounds, does hearing persist or not?*
> *It does.*
> *When there are sounds, it follows that we hear them, but how can hearing take place during the absence of sound?*
> *We are now talking of that hearing which is independent of there being any sound or not. How*

> *can that be? The nature of hearing being eternal, we continue to hear whether sounds are present or not.*
> *If that is so, who or what is the hearer?*
> *It is your own nature which hears and it is the inner cognizer who knows.*[1]

'Your own nature, the inner cognizer,' said Hui Hai, 'hears and knows.' 'Your own nature, the inner cognizer' — he means something other than thoughts and that which is produced by thoughts, and he means something other than the body.

Many people understand instinctively they are more than just flesh and blood and mental processes, yet they cannot make any sense of it intellectually and fail to recognize it on a conscious level.

It is easy to see how thoughts, sensations, and whatever else is perceived arise and pass away, and how the body changes. This arising and passing away is birth and death. The unborn, that which is aware of this arising and passing away, however, does not come into being and does not cease to be.

Is the unborn eternal, then? Does it last forever? Do 'I' as the unborn last forever? It cannot be said that the unborn is eternal either, because it has never come into

[1] *The Zen Teaching of Instantaneous Awakening*, Hui Hai, trans. John Blofeld, Buddhist Publishing Group, 1987.

unborn is eternal either, because it has never come into existence; it isn't anything which can be thought of in those terms, or in any terms at all; it just *is*.

The mind and body may be seen as either a single unit, or as a combination of parts — form, sensation, perception, mental activity and consciousness. These five parts, changing constantly yet holding together are what in intellectual terms may be regarded as a sentient being. The body moves about, gets hungry, tired and sick; it grows, matures, becomes old and wrinkled, decays. Mental and physical sensations turn from pleasure to pain and from pain to pleasure again purely on a sensual level. Experiences are perceived as good and bad, and then as good again on an intellectual and emotional level. Thoughts come, stay for a fleeting moment, and then go again. Consciousness of one thing is experienced, and then of something else, and then of something else, and so it goes on — mind and body — the same yet not the same from moment to moment, different yet not different, nothing permanent to be found anywhere, nothing to be construed as 'self'. Yet 'I' do not go anywhere! This we can call rebirth.

Rebirth

Whatever comes into being must pass away again — a breath, a sound, a smell, a taste, a touch, a thought, a torment, a moment of beauty, a life . . .

Coming to be and passing away, continuously, like the ebb and flow of the tide — nothing is gained, nothing lost. This is a little truth with a great significance in the life of a human being. The passing away of one thing brings something else into existence. Yet the passing away of the one and the coming to be of the other has no dividing line between them, no gap. As I walk from the house to the garden, I leave the realm of the house. The people in the house see me go; they see me die to the house. As I enter the garden, the people there see my birth into their world. For me, I have not experienced any death or birth, only a change in conditions.

The passing away, or dying, of one state is the birth of another, but the moment remains the same. The threshold is crossed without any movement taking place; leaving and entering occur simultaneously — no sense of having lost oneself in the process. 'Births' and 'deaths' are no more than evolutions, spirals, and developments.

Change has never been experienced as annihilation by anyone, and yet so many believe in death as the final blackout! Others believe just as vehemently in permanent states of being, such as heavens or hells. But what is the truth? Do I die? I experience this body and mind, and the world of this body and mind, and I will experience the breakdown of this body and mind, but will I die? Will the essence of what I am cease to be? In order to die, I first must be born. But have I been born? This is the crux of the matter.

You may think that at death you will transmigrate — seek and find another birth here in this world. Or you may think you will go to sleep forever — finished! You may think beings are real, permanent, unchanging. Or you may think that life is all just illusion. You may think many things, but it's all just thought; it doesn't mean a thing.

With views and opinions cleared away, with preconceived ideas unproduced, with what is presented in life now and nothing added, you see the moment for what it is — as neither past nor future, neither eternal nor subject to annihilation. You may see it as timeless or as all time. When the mind is settled and clear, you become aware of stillness contrasted by movement; you become aware of the energy of life; you become aware of the rebecoming process.

While Meichee Patomwon was on retreat, meditating in her Thai Buddhist monastery twenty-nine years ago, her whole body suddenly filled with pain. It was an intense pain which lasted for three hours. The pain then suddenly vanished as if someone had come along and pulled out her heart, her feelings. After that her body felt so light that she had to open her eyes to see if she still had hands, arms and legs. At this moment the thought of rebirth occurred to her; she felt that this was the recollection of a previous life.

For the next six months Meichee Patomwon continued meditating intensely in silence within the confines of the monastery. In this meditative state it seemed to her that there was no man, no woman, no one, no individual, just emptiness. She had a whole range of different experiences at this time. She felt as though she was watching a film. Voices, visions and memories arose in her heart.

After six months in retreat, she set out to see whether there was any truth in the visions she had experienced, and whether a name that had come to her was of any significance. She found the village that had come to her in her visions, a place she had never visited before. She came to the house and soon discovered that the name was of great significance for it belonged to the man who lived there.

Meichee Patomwon recounted to the man and his wife what had come to her in the meditation experience; she spoke of the last moments of what she regarded as her previous life, the very time of death when the mother and father were present. The couple couldn't believe it as they heard this stranger recounting the details of the death of their three-month old baby daughter some twenty-two years earlier. All accepted this to be a genuine case of rebirth.

If this were true, then Meichee Patomwon in a previous life had died at three months old when the mother was eighteen. The gap between her death and conception in this life was ten months. The mother of the last life is now in her mid-sixties and the mother of this life is in her seventies, so there is no big age difference between them.

Meichee Patomwon is now forty-eight and both mothers have taken ordination in the same monastery at which she is head nun. In fact, Meichee Patomwon is head nun of the province and is a greatly respected speaker on spirituality and meditation. But when she recounts her story, she is filled with sadness because she says, 'It seems that there is no ending of us.' She feels that we just go round and round and round and round —

birth, death, birth, death, in a never ending cycle, a life-cycle of happiness and unhappiness.

'It is good to see,' she says, 'how unsatisfactory things can be, then you don't get distracted; you don't forget and get carried away. It is good to see how suffering arises and passes away.'

And she goes on to say, 'There is more suffering than happiness in this life. Ending the suffering is experiencing real happiness, and this is not the happiness you get when you acquire something you want; it is the happiness, the real happiness, the real joy of coming to the end of suffering. If you know how to bring unsatisfactoriness to an end, then you will know how to experience the real bliss of existence.'

It is good to see how suffering arises and passes away.

To her, rebirth from body and mind to body and mind is a fact, and she needs no proof of it, but that does not fill her with joy. On the contrary, as far as she is concerned, the most important thing in life is to break free of body and mind, for that is how real happiness is to be found.

Liberation from suffering and genuine deep happiness, for Meichee Patomwon, does not lie in the thought that she has lived in a previous life and may proceed to a future one; instead it is in freeing herself from the physical and mental realm altogether.

Escaping Rebirth

O ne of the main things which fascinated me about Eastern religions as a teenager was the doctrine of rebirth or reincarnation and other realms of being — not just one life, but many! How fair! Much fairer than having to put up with a single miserable existence of an indeterminate length, full of woe and injustice, which so many people and animals obviously have to do. And after that — what? Heaven? Or hell? Forever! Or nothing at all? Could it be that all that struggling and suffering is for nothing?

If death were a doorway to a new life, on the other hand, it could be welcomed as an opportunity for something better, or so I thought at that time, 'better' being exciting experiences and happiness, of course, in a sort of feeling or materialistic sense.

When I first came across the idea of escaping birth and death, I brushed it aside. What did the Buddha say? 'There is an unborn, an unageing, an undying. If there were not this unborn, there would be no escape from birth, ageing and death.' Escaping birth, ageing and death? Escaping birth? Escaping being reborn next time?

But I'd only just got used to the idea that there would be a next time and now I was to escape it! That thought didn't appeal to me at all. I somehow felt that escaping birth must be almost like being annihilated — no body, no mind, no self — just a nebulous sort of 'nonbeing', whatever that was!

Even though Buddhism professed not to be nihilistic in any way, therefore, I still associated escaping birth and death with a form of nihilism, and if liberation and enlightenment meant a sort of annihilation, I rather preferred to remain a little ignorant so that existence would continue for me and the ones I loved! And yet there was something in me which didn't want to ignore the truth whatever it might be, and so I meditated with great vigour.

It took me many years to realize that the rise and fall of sensations, perceptions, thoughts, and varying states of consciousness were in fact births and deaths — rebirths. But more and more I did realize it as a living reality. Spontaneous uprisings of the moment — the moment itself being a spontaneous uprising — that was rebirth in all its glory, and it was a very obvious fact. Why hadn't I noticed it before? With that, however, came another realization, something just as obvious as the first. Rebirths (births and deaths of phenomena) are what take place all the while. But *where* do they take place? Does phenomena arise inside me, or do I come into being inside of phenomena?

It is our custom to think of ourselves as little units arising within an already constructed universe. To see it from a different angle, however, has an interesting effect. When the mind is calm and the inner eye of awareness is wide open, it is possible to suddenly see form (mental as well as physical) within the nonmaterial, the 'me to myself'. Seeing the nonmaterial, unborn, unmade, unformed as the space inside which life takes place is encountering no birth, no ageing, and no dying. Suddenly 'I' am the formless as well as the form. Notions of 'me and my life' at this point do not apply. To see that is to realize that escaping rebirth is to lose nothing except entanglement in a lot of heartache and suffering.

Rebirth, therefore, is to be recognized as a process occurring in the moment, whether the body is functioning strongly, or is breaking down at death. Whatever comes into being ceases to be. And yet 'coming to be and ceasing to be', 'birth and death', 'rebirth', 'inside and outside' are just labels, products of the thinking mind and nothing more. Liberation from thought, therefore, and the contracted mind and heart which accompanies it is liberation from rebirth in a very deep sense.

The Things We Do

There is something within our lives that we don't normally recognize as being other than the body and its processes. We do not distinguish that which is operating within us which takes no form whatsoever. It is here inside of us, but we fail to see it; we are psychologically blind to something which is closer than our thoughts and feelings, closer than our bodies. If we can spot it amidst all those emotions, bodily sensations and dreams we call life, the entire universe would be transformed.

'Me' and nature — what is the difference? 'Me' and the forces which move the universe — what is the difference? Misery and exaltation — what is the difference? Praise and blame — what is the difference? Pleasure and pain — what is the difference? Do you want pleasure? Do you spend your life seeking it? Do you spend your life trying to avoid pain? Do you contravene the laws of nature? Do you contravene the laws which govern you and all things? Contravening natural forces is as futile as trying to stop a bolt of lightning with the palm of your hand. Have you ever stopped a bolt of lightning with the palm of your hand? Have you ever stopped Monday morning? Were you able to stop the one you loved from dying?

Life hurts, doesn't it, in so many ways? And it's important to know that. But, wait a minute, do you ever hurt life? Have you ever hurt anything or anyone? Have you ever wilfully damaged anything or any other being in any way? Has your heart ever broken for the things you have done, or not done? Have you ever damaged the moment by wishing it were different? Ask yourself these questions.

Do you want to hurt others? Some people do, don't they? They derive extraordinary pleasure from obscene acts of cruelty. But it is my belief that whoever goes deeply enough into their own hearts and minds will feel a horrible revulsion for all those ugly thoughts and deeds. I find I don't like myself much for the nasty things I've done. I find it leaves me with a nauseating feeling in the pit of my stomach.

There can't be many people who are able to look into the mirror and congratulate themselves for being sods, that is if they admit it in the first place. Do you like yourself? If you don't, you can't expect others to like you, either. Why should anyone else find beautiful that which you find ugly? But can you forgive yourself for all those nasty little things that you've done? Can you start anew every moment? Can you accept other people for what they are and forgive them, irrespective of what they think of you? It's a strange thing, but it seems that we can only love others to the extent that we can love ourselves. Is there a difference between 'you' and 'me'?

It seems that our nature is to love, to have compassion for all beings. Not to do so is painful — it hurts. Not to have compassion is, in itself, an act of violence beyond compare — torturous. And the mind becomes disturbed on a very deep level. But what about when a person is just not nice? What about those who try to cheat us, hurt us, cause us to suffer pain and torture and untold misery? What about the pigs who rape old ladies, the soldiers who torture their victims with great skill and ingenuity? Is it possible to love them? Certainly not in the conventional sense. And I have no desire to be at one with them in any sense, but they are a part of me whether I like it or not. I cannot expel them from the universe, from their existence in my mind. We are one, me and those pigs!

There is something at play in compassion which has absolutely nothing to do with what a person is like, or what he or she has done, however abominable. Compassion is a force within oneself which lets everything pass by without judgement. That is love of another order. It is unlimited by space or time and makes no distinctions. It is a way of being which asks no questions and gives no answers and lets nature take its course.

We can live by all sorts of religious disciplines and moral codes if we like, but we have our own moral code deep inside. And in my opinion that is the real one. The first thing is to find it; the second is to live by it. And then it's a glorious life — still full of pleasure and pain, praise and blame, but glorious to the core.

We want to love our lives; we want it desperately. We need to be happy with what we've got and with what we find here. After all, this is all there is. But we can only live by what we find and know for ourselves, not by what someone else finds. Nor can we impose our world upon others. Each person's life is unique. A rose is a rose; it isn't a daisy. A daffodil is a daffodil; a geranium is a geranium. They are all flowers, we are all people, but each one is quite different and has a beauty of its own. That is the way it is. No one's life is right or wrong; it is what it is for that person.

Occasionally, of course, we may come across someone who doesn't appear to have anything beautiful about him or her at all. Well, if we locate the source of our own being — it isn't far away — and live from that, we shall find we are not contravening the laws of nature and stabbing ourselves in the chest by the things we think, say and do in relation to that person.

Inside of us the universe flows unhindered, but we make pathetic attempts at rejecting it with anger, jealousy, greed, ill will, sorrow and misery. The universe flows on, but somehow we don't want to flow with it. That is suffering, and it is karma in action. *We* want to go one way, the universe goes another and we are torn apart in the process. We fight ourselves. There is no outside force attacking us. There is no outside! We hurt ourselves.

I used to work in the office of an engineering factory many years ago in Leicester. Sometimes I would have to walk through the factory where hundreds of men worked building woodworking and metalworking equipment. The noise would be so great with all the machinery going at the same time that you would have to scream at the top of your voice to the person standing next to you, or else you wouldn't be heard. And if you didn't like that cacophony of sound and screwed up your face and put your hands to your ears, it did no good at all. That was in the days before ear defenders and I am sure most of the men who worked in that factory became partially deaf not long after they took up employment. But for someone like me who didn't go onto the factory floor very often, the noise was an assault to the ears. Eventually I discovered, in that factory, that if I didn't offer up any resistance to the sound and just allowed it to roar through me, it wasn't a bad sensation at all; in fact, I discovered, there was something rather stimulating and pleasant about it. After that I rather looked forward to going into that noisy place, and have enjoyed other noisy places ever since.

I and the clamour of that machinery became one; the noise vibrated through me without resistance and did me no harm. There are limits, of course, and I am sure I would wear the ear-defenders if I had to work in such places for long especially if I wanted to protect the quality of my hearing, but sometimes it is quite easy to make friends with sensations, circumstances and beings that come to us. To reject what comes to us, it seems to me, is to reject ourselves, because what comes to us is meant for us in that moment, otherwise it would not be there! I do not believe the universe makes mistakes.

To be totally free of everything is to be totally at one with everything. It's a paradox! Attached to this body by desire and mysterious forces, walking around as it, suffering as it, the unborn 'me' never comes to birth. There is no division between me and other things and beings when I never come to birth, and I don't hit myself over the head with negative feelings and mental and physical illnesses brought on by hating and despising what I see and hear and touch during the course of a normal day.

Many little messages come through from the universe in the form of dreams, negative states of mind, irritations and so forth to tell us something. These are reactions, kickbacks from the greater part of ourselves; they are the actions of karma rectifying the balance in a most mysterious and unfathomable way. It is worth taking notice of these little messages. They are, after all, meant for us. The way things happen by nature, 'me', and the things 'I' do — are all just one.

Look. Look closely as you live and breathe, touch, and speak. Where is the other? Inside you or outside, or in neither place? Watch and wait, and abandon all idea of 'me watching'. See the same truths appear again and again in different guises, each time with a deeper significance. Look at the things you do and what happens in consequence. Release the tension in the abdomen. Breathe freely.

Feel the Sensation

There is incredible beauty in moving the body, touching things, picking them up, carrying them from place to place, washing dishes, polishing wood and metal, placing ink on paper, smoothing the creases with an iron, looking at someone openly. It is extraordinary, but even the simplest of tasks embodies the greatest spiritual happiness when performed calmly and with a quiet mind. We are free to enjoy what we do, free to see the patterns, to hear the music in all things when nothing is yearned for.

'But,' you may say, 'I haven't got the time; I have to do things in such a rush — the house, the kids, the job. I haven't got time to see the incredible beauty in washing the pots. Have you seen that pile over there?'

How *is* one able to do a job calmly and in one's own time when there are so many things to do? Pay full attention to what you are doing and let the body move. It will be the greatest of joys. Don't do a job just to get it done even if you have to rush; that's a waste! Do it with all of your being. Do it for its own sake and know time — the time to begin, the time to end, the time to wait, the time to go.

Stretch out your hand and touch an object very gently and with great sensitivity. Feel the sensation in your hand and arm and the whole of your body. Let the division between you and the things you touch disappear. Learn to love movement and contact, sound and colour.

Things turn out badly sometimes. That is the way the universe works. Living is a precarious business; most people are crushed by it at some point in their lives, if not all of their lives. They think pleasure is good and pain is bad. But it is better to recognize the true self and the nature of this moment, and to realize there is nothing to crush.

There is a very easy pattern to life. If you stay with the moment, there is just enough time to do what needs to be done, just enough materials to complete the job as far as it needs completing. And if the time has run out and panic sets in, well, that can be interesting too. Smile a little. Not every demand for your attention needs to be gratified. Not every letter needs a reply. Not every offer should be accepted. The body goes to what is right, does what is right. If truth is your purpose, the mind will inevitably incline towards it.

Be aware of the breath entering and leaving the body. Look at the rise and fall of the abdomen. Look at the body walking in silence. Look at others walking by. Listen without desire. Look at the mind. Look at pleasure. Look at pain. Open the inner eye and see this very moment, now. Sense life, smell it, taste it, listen to it directly with the very core of your being. The mundane will become profound.

If boredom comes, brush it aside; don't attach to it; it is another condition of the mind which distorts the truth. The moment is not dull and boring; only the mind makes it so. If pain comes, let it be. There is something painless in the heart of being and the essence of the moment. If agitation comes, let it settle. Trying to force calmness will only create further agitation. In a quieter moment take the opportunity to return to the source of your being.

There can be no end to insight, so many are the ways of experiencing the same thing. As one draws closer to an object it changes its form. There is no need to go anywhere or do anything to plumb the depths of the universe and one's own being.

Enjoy washing that pile of pots!

The Way

Happiness cannot be forced into existence, nor can it be forced out of it, but it can be held in abeyance. That is what we do when we hang on to things and people and ideas in our minds and refuse to let them go. The mind becomes blocked like a plughole full of potato peelings, and the way is dammed up.

Being alert, observing the movements of the mind and body in daily life, noticing what is taking place as opposed to what one wishes would take place, or what one fears might take place, or what one grieves over as having already taken place is a way of life which is completely free of all self-imposed restrictions and conflicting states of mind. Wisdom and compassion will be allowed to function freely under these circumstances.

Views, speech, ways of living, mindfulness and concentration are unhindered by greed, guilt, hatred, carelessness, complacency, and fear when divisions are seen to be arbitrary and there is no sense of, 'This is me;' 'That is you.'

When the way ahead is open and clear and one has the good will, light-heartedness, and courage to tread it, the past and the future melt into nothingness, life is lived from the centre of one's being, and the self becomes as meaningful as the blue sky, the green fields, the flowing rivers, the polluted atmosphere, the littered streets, the hustling crowds, the filth and the beauty.

When one follows what is right according to one's heart and good sense, when wisdom and compassion become real, not contrived, the magical way of heaven manifests beneath one's feet. That is the way of liberation from suffering and the realization of genuine happiness.

Other
BPG
Publications

Other BPG Publications

AN INTRODUCTION TO BUDDHISM
Ed. Diana St.Ruth

A comprehensive account of Buddhism and its teachings. Advice on treading the Buddhist path, with easy-to-follow instructions on how to meditate, also make this a practical guide for those who wish to experience the truth of what the Buddha taught.
0-946672-22-9

TEACHINGS OF A BUDDHIST MONK
Ajahn Sumedho Foreword by Jack Kornfield

Ajahn Sumedho invites us all, ordained and lay people alike, to enjoy the freedom beyond all conditions, a freedom from fears, from gain and loss, from pleasure and pain.
0-946672-23-7

THE ZEN TEACHING OF
INSTANTANEOUS AWAKENING
Hui Hai   Trans. John Blofeld

An eighth-century T'ang Dynasty Zen Text. Zen Master Hui Hai was of the same spiritual tradition as Hui Neng, Ma Tsu and Huang Po. His style of teaching is very direct and just as pertinent today in the West as it was twelve hundred years ago in China. 'When things happen,' says Hui Hai, 'make no response: keep your minds from dwelling on anything whatsoever: keep them for ever still as the void and utterly pure (without stain): and thereby spontaneously attain deliverance.'
0-946672-03-2

FINGERS AND MOONS
Trevor Leggett

A collection of humorous and instructive Zen stories and incidents pointing directly to the truth in ourselves.
0-946672-07-5

ZEN GRAFFITI
Azuki

A book of aphorisms and robust line drawings which point to the practice and fruits of Buddhism. They can nudge one out of apathy, dullness and habit into a direct awareness of the moment's reality. Each reader will respond to different sayings according to individual need and development.

0-946672-24-5

PERFECT WISDOM:
The Short Prajñāpāramitā Texts
Translated by Edward Conze

This book contains some of the most profound holy texts ever written, including Perfection of Wisdom in 500 Lines, Perfection of Wisdom in 700 Lines, Heart Sutra, and Diamond Sutra. These texts offer guidance to all those interested in the Great Wisdom.

0-946672-28-8

THE BUDDHA'S LAW AMONG THE BIRDS
Translated by Edward Conze

Some three hundred years ago an unknown lama wrote this charming little book describing how the birds of the Himalayas met on a holy mountain under the leadership of the great Bodhisattva Avalokitesvara who had taken the form of a cuckoo. Who taught them how to live a Buddhist way of life.

0-946672-29-6

BVDDHISM NOW

A quarterty Buddhist journal - interviews, practical advice on living a Buddhist way of life, translations, stories, verse, letters, news, book reviews etc. (Send £1 or $2 for a sample issue.)